The Problem with the Seventh Year

Nicholas Pierpan

I0192798

methuen | drama

LONDON • NEW YORK • OXFORD • NEW DELHI • SYDNEY

METHUEN DRAMA

Bloomsbury Publishing Plc, 50 Bedford Square, London, WC1B 3DP, UK
Bloomsbury Publishing Inc, 1359 Broadway, New York, NY 10018, USA
Bloomsbury Publishing Ireland, 29 Earlsfort Terrace, Dublin 2, D02 AY28, Ireland

BLOOMSBURY, METHUEN DRAMA and the Methuen
Drama logo are trademarks of Bloomsbury Publishing Plc

First published in Great Britain 2025

Copyright © Nicholas Pierpan, 2025

Nicholas Pierpan has asserted their right under the Copyright, Designs and Patents
Act, 1988, to be identified as Author of this work.

Photograph: Colin Thomas
Cover design: Briar Knowles

A catalogue record for this book is available from the British Library.

A catalog record for this book is available from the Library of Congress.

ISBN: PB: 978-1-3506-1587-8
         ePDF: 978-1-3506-1588-5
         eBook: 978-1-3506-1589-2

Series: Modern Plays

Typeset by Westchester Publishing Services

For product safety related questions contact productsafety@bloomsbury.com.

To find out more about our authors and books visit
www.bloomsbury.com and sign up for our newsletters.

19th Street Productions in association with
White Bear Theatre presents

The London Premiere

The Problem with the Seventh Year

by **Nicholas Pierpan**

First performed as *The Cutman* at Theatre Ulm,
Germany, 24 October 2009.

First performance at the White Bear Theatre
28 October 2025.

Cast

Man	**James McGregor**
Director	**Paul O'Mahony**
Lighting Designer	**Will Hayman**
Sound Designer	**Raffaela Pancucci**
Stage Manager	**Ryan Kingsbury**
Producer	**Sarah Roy**

James McGregor

Man

James has an MA in Drama and Theatre Arts from the University of Birmingham, and went on to train in acting at the Bristol Old Vic Theatre School. His credits include:

Theatre: *Did You Mean to Fall Like That* (Pleasance, Edinburgh); *Bacchanalia* (site-specific/Sleepwalk Immersive); *Harry Potter and the Cursed Child* (The Palace Theatre); *Rage, But Hope* (Edinburgh/London run); *The Indian Queen* (Opera de Lille); *Henry I of England* (site-specific/Reading Between The Lines); *Merlin* (Nuffield, Southampton); *Other Desert Cities* (English Theatre, Frankfurt); *The Final Revelation of Sherlock Holmes* (The Pleasance); *Robin Hood* (The Globe/Borough Market); *Profumo: The Musical* (Waterloo East); *Dinner* (Barons Court Theatre); *A Midsummer Night's Dream* (The Globe/Borough Market); *The Hairy Ape* (Southwark Playhouse); *The Alchemist* (White Bear); *The Merchant of Venice* (Rose Theatre); *Hamlet Smith* (Southwark Nursery Festival); *The Eight: Reindeer Monologues* (Above The Stag); *Palace Balls* (Jermyn Street).

TV: *EastEnders*, *Call the Midwife*, *Here We Go*, *Casualty*, *Our World War*, *The Great Train Robbery* and *Waking the Dead* (BBC); *FBI International* (HBO); *Silo* (Apple TV); *Kiss of Death* (Discovery); *Emmerdale* and *Foyle's War* (ITV); *Land of the Free* (History); *Angel of Decay* and *Obsession: Dark Desire* (Discovery ID); *Miracle Landing on the Hudson* (NatGeo).

Film: *Pride*, *Cerberus*, *The Cocktail Waitress* and *Stu (Stuart) & Ollie* pts.1, 2 & 3.

Computer Game: *As Dusk Falls* (Xbox/Int-Night).

Nicholas Pierpan

Playwright

Nicholas Pierpan is a playwright and screenwriter. *The Problem with the Seventh Year* won the Cameron Mackintosh Award for New Writing. Nicholas won the 2013 Off West End Award for Most Promising Playwright and was nominated for an Evening Standard Award for his play *You Can Still Make a Killing*. He has won two Peggy Ramsay Awards, and was shortlisted for the Yale Drama Prize. He was selected for the BBC Drama Production Writers' Scheme and won the Script Factory Serious Screenwriting Award. After a BBC Sparks Radio Residency, Nicholas's radio plays have been broadcast on BBC3, BBC4 and BBC6. He was named on the BBC's New Talent Hotlist in 2017, and in 2020/21 was a member of the Serial Eyes programme for television writers at the DFFB in Berlin. He now lives in London, where he teaches creative writing at Royal Holloway, University of London.

Paul O'Mahony
Director

Paul O'Mahony is a director, actor and writer.

As artistic director of Out of Chaos he has devised, written and performed *Out of Chaos*, *Unmythable*, *Norsesome*, *Is Now A Good Time?* and *There's Something Going On Here*. Out of Chaos's productions have won awards at major festivals in England, Germany, Scotland and Spain. Their production of *Macbeth* recently toured the UK to critical acclaim and will be touring nationally and internationally in 2026.

Other acting credits include several seasons at the Orange Tree Theatre; *Othello* (RSC); *The Taming of the Shrew* (Plymouth Theatre Royal); *Suppliants* (Battersea Arts Centre); *Ice* (English Touring Opera); *Next Door* (Out of Balanz, Denmark).

He wrote and directed *A History of Sound* for Vache Baroque, and will be directing their production of *The Tempest* in August 2026. Other directing credits include *Unmythable* (Out of Chaos); *The Suppliants* (EU Center, Illinois) and *Iphigenia* (BADA).

Will Hayman
Lighting Designer

Will is a UK-based lighting designer and chief electrician at Oxford Playhouse. He has trained with the National Youth Theatre, was awarded a place on the Association of Lighting Designers' Lumiere scheme in 2020, and was in 2023 nominated for an Offie Award. In 2025, his lighting design for *Scatter* won *Theatre Weekly*'s Best Design (Set/Costume/Lighting) at the Edinburgh Festival Fringe.

Previous lighting designs include: *Babies* (The Other Palace); *Coming to England* (UK tour); *Scatter* (Underbelly Edinburgh, Underbelly Boulevard); *Max Fosh: Loophole* (Hammersmith Apollo, UK and international tour); *Sleeping Beauty* (The Oxford Playhouse); *Max Fosh Zocial Butterfly* (London Palladium, Clapham Grand, McEwan Hall Edinburgh, UK tour); *Colossal* (Soho Theatre, Underbelly Edinburgh); *SORTED Live: The Big Christmas Bash* (Shoreditch Town Hall) and many others.

Raffaela Pancucci
Sound Designer

Raffaela trained in Theatre Sound at the Royal Central School of Speech and Drama.

As sound designer: *lenny.* (The Omnibus Theatre); *1:17 AM, or until the words run out* (Theatre503); *1972: The Future of Sex* (The Webber Douglas Theatre); *Marshmallow Me* (The Harlow Playhouse and UK tour); *Basic Bald B*tch* (Brixton House); *Last Black Girl on Earth* (Camden Roundhouse); *Pippin*, *Earthquakes in London* (The Backstage Theatre, Mountview); *Invisible Animal*, *Phaedra* (The Omnibus Theatre); *Then, Now & Next* (Southwark Playhouse); *BEASTS, or why girls shouldn't fear the dark* (ZOO Playground Edinburgh, The Omnibus Theatre); *Choose Your Fighter* (Camden People's Theatre); *Please Feel Free to Share* (Pleasance Attic Edinburgh, King's Head Theatre, Theatre503); *This Last Piece of Sky* (The Space Arts Centre); *The Boy with the Bee Jar* (The Hope Theatre); *Piaf, The Yellow Wallpaper* (The Catford Broadway Studio Theatre) and *Man Muck* (The Etcetera Theatre).

Ryan Kingsbury
Stage Manager

Ryan is a lighting and sound designer, programmer and technician based in London. He works primarily at the White Bear Theatre. Credits include: *Eh, Up Me Old Flowers* (2025); *Switcheroo* (2025); *Candy* (2025); *The Work We Do* (2024); *Burden of Proof* (2024); *A Weekend Away at the Hotel Decevoir* (2024); *We Weren't Innocent* (2024); *The Adam Error* (2024); *Just Call Me Al* (2024); *BESA* and *A Rude Awokening* (2024).

Sarah Roy
Producer

Sarah Roy trained as an actor at the American Academy of Dramatic Arts, New York before founding 19th Street Productions. She produced and performed the one woman show, *Catherine and Anita* (Edinburgh Fringe Festival (Assembly Rooms) and Kings Head Theatre). The script was then adapted into the feature film, *Zebra Girl*, which she produced, co-wrote and starred in alongside Tom Cullen and Jade Anouka. *Zebra Girl* was nominated for Best Thriller at the National Film Awards. Sarah then produced the critically acclaimed *Yes So I Said Yes* by David Ireland followed by *Not Now* (both at the Finborough Theatre). *Not Now* was included in *The Observer*'s Top 10 shows of 2022.

Sarah was associate producer of the Tony Award winning musical *A Strange Loop* at The Barbican in 2023.

She is producing David Ireland's new play *Most Favoured* at the Soho Theatre in December 2025.

Production Acknowledgements

The Problem with the Seventh Year is supported using public funding from the National Lottery through Arts Council England, and also by the generous donations of our supporters. Thank you to Thomas and Jennifer Pierpan, Chris and Deanna Pierpan, Andrew Pierpan and Elizabeth Sarma, Henry and Monica Pierpan, Sara Pierpan Urrutia and Kevin Urrutia, Gary Beestone, Linda Baker, Magdalena Alvarez Icaza Jackson, Joanne Taylor, Daniel Anixt, Peter McDonald, Catrin Barnsteiner, Wyndham Albery and Sarah Churchwell, Acely Garza, Mark Williams, Philip O'Mahony, Steve Jarvis, Dave Crellin, John Palmer, Jonathan George, Erica Charters, Gillian Hamnett and William Wood, Natalie Rule, Ian Huish, Jim McCue, Ashley Campbell, Beau Hopkins and Contemporary Ritual Theatre, Lu Herbert, Grace Carley and Tony De Meur.

Supported using public funding by

**ARTS COUNCIL
ENGLAND**

LOTTERY FUNDED

The multi-award winning White Bear Theatre was founded by Michael Kingsbury in 1989 and has helped develop some of the country's leading theatre makers including Joe Penhall, Sharon Horgan and Dennis Kelly. It has also hosted work by a new generation of practitioners including Ruby Thomas, Polaroid Theatre, Blanche McIntyre, The Ugly Sisters and Martha Watson Allpress.

The White Bear Theatre has received numerous awards including Timeout Best Fringe Theatre, Peter Brook – Empty Space Award for Best Fringe Theatre. And Best Ensemble. The Off-West End Award for Best Director, Best Actor and Best Actress in the public vote. The founder and Artistic director received the London Pub Theatre Award for Outstanding Contribution to Pub Theatre in November 2022.

West End and number one touring transfers include *Round the Horne . . . Re-visited* (The Leicester Square Theatre); *Maggie and Ted* (Garrick Theatre); *Dom* (The Other Palace and Theatre Royal Windsor); *Viva Espana* (The Arts); *Jumping the Shark* (number one tour).

Follow Us Online

www.facebook.com/WhiteBearTheatre

www.x.com/WhiteBearTheatr

www.instagram.com/whitebeartheatre/?hl=en

The Problem with the Seventh Year

Characters

MAN

MAN

When you put on the gloves, you take them off. Each in his own way – there's the aging heavyweight who takes them off after boxing every day of his life since he was six, and there's the smarmy teenager who spars once in the local gym and quits.

Maybe he got his nose broken. Maybe not. Each in his own way.

But the heavyweight quits too.

(*Silence.*)

Did you know more movies have been made about boxing than all other sports put together? It's a fact. People like to watch stories about boxing. What do they want to know? What do they want to see? What's so goddamn important it can't be seen simply watching a boxing match?

A good bout says it all, and is almost as long as a movie. I mean, professionals fight ten or twelve rounds every bout. Sometimes fifteen.

You fight fifteen rounds, three minutes each, one minute between rounds, the bout lasts fifty-nine minutes.

An hour. Well, fifty-nine minutes.

I always thought they should fit one more minute in, somewhere.

I thought if you fight a man toe-to-toe for a full hour, what does the outcome matter?

You could die happy. The rest doesn't mean anything.

Because you see, a punch takes less than a second to throw. You can throw three big punches in one second. Put that into an hour. Do the math. You see the numbers on the

4 The Problem with the Seventh Year

television: someone got hit by Joe Frazier 260 times over twelve rounds.

They tell you that but it doesn't mean anything. It's like someone telling you the sun is twenty million miles in diameter. You can't really understand it.

The sun is right there in front of you, but you can't see it.

Imagine what *fifteen rounds* is like with Frazier. Actually, don't.

You can't that's why.

You can only be in awe of the idea.

But what they don't talk about, in the movies or anywhere else, is the deeper beauty of it. The fact is, the boxer who got hit by Joe Frazier 260 times didn't really feel it, either. Sure, he felt the first few punches, and some of the big ones, but mostly he was afraid of the idea of getting hit by Joe Frazier far more than he minded actually getting hit by him.

Once he got hit, it was over. Didn't matter, no big deal.

That's the nature of boxing. The way it is. That's what makes it a beautiful sport.

Afterwards you wonder what you were so scared of. But you go to sleep and the next day you wake up and you've got to go back down to the gym and you're scared of getting hit again. Think about it all day. Then it's late afternoon, you're down the gym, you get in there, take a few, and it's all right.

You don't care for a little while, at least until you sleep again. That's the good thing about boxing. The good side.

The bad side is . . . well, you've got to hit them back.

You can't be nice.

You can't be polite and hope for the best.

You got to throw every punch with 'bad intentions.' If you don't, you're better off becoming an educated gentleman and not a boxer.

And don't kid yourself: you can't be both.

They just don't go together, I'm telling you.

I mean, there's a reason all the great fighters come from the ghetto. They may be smart, brilliant fighters, but they're not educated in the proper, conventional ways.

They don't read books, and they don't think like them either. And that's to their credit.

If there's something to be said for boxing, it's that.

Those fighters know something else, that others don't. Or maybe it's what they don't know.

Something to do with fear. The fear of consequence.

(*Silence.*)

I don't know how cutmen do it.

I really don't. Fuck the stories about boxing: cutmen are more interesting, they see a lot more, they *see* it.

And it's not easy for them, trust me. In its own way, it was easier just being a boxer.

(*Bell rings/light change.*)

Was I a nice boy? Was I educated 'properly'? I don't know. There was evidence on both sides, but I won't bore you.

I tried to be a nice boy and, at times, I tried not to be a nice boy. Very deliberate. Neither attempts very successful, I think.

I was bright. For that part of town, those schools, I was bright. That said, most of the people I knew weren't very interested in intellectual pursuit: the most popular academic subjects were trying to fix cars that didn't work, stealing cars that *did* work, and 'the sweet science.'

My brother saw me getting interested in the other things, and that's why he took me down the gym.

The nose was the first to go. Took less than a week. I wanted to quit, but I figured once you break your nose, badly, who cares? So I wouldn't be pretty. Nothing worse could happen. That's when I still had all my teeth.

I was bright. They wanted to put me in special classes. I wasn't so sure, but I didn't speak up when I should have. I nodded, they smiled – I wanted to leave the room and it seemed the quickest way. They made me uncomfortable, those smiles.

Like they cared really. Really? I would make them look good. Or something. There was some real purpose involved.

They sent me away to another, special school in western Massachusetts. Then I moved to Worcester for university. Worcester is the second biggest city in New England, but no one ever hears about it. Because it's a shithole, that's why, a real cesspool. It was once richer than Boston.

Things were different there. I had lots of classes. Studied medicine. There was a good coach there, and I boxed at his gym.

But there were problems. I had problems paying attention in class. Once, I passed out in a lecture.

I wasn't eating much.

It's not that I couldn't afford to eat, you see I didn't want to eat.

I enjoyed the hunger. Something you only feel when it's all the time.

And I was dropping weight. Fast. I wanted to be the tallest light middleweight in the entire city. I wanted to be the tallest light middleweight that city'd ever seen!

It was not long afterwards that I met Gregory.

He was my second bout. Knocked me out in the first. I remember it. Just before it started we met with the referee in the middle of the ring, and we're asked to touch gloves – Gregory just looks up at me, smiles, and says 'good luck.'

Scared the shit out of me.

So I went after him, and he knocked me out. Straight right to the chin . . . I think.

I got up. But that was it. I didn't lose another fight the rest of that year. Five amateur fights and I won them all. I was happy.

But Gregory.

He was just the second fight I'd had in that city and he knocked me out. You remember that.

You remember that. In the streets. You know he lives in the city, and when you go into a bar, or a garage, you're always thinking for some reason that he'll be there. Pop out from behind the corner or something.

But I never saw Gregory.

I wasn't looking, but I didn't find him either.

One thing though, I didn't like walking around knowing someone out there could beat me up.

The point is I didn't have to wait long. I saw him again, in the traditional way.

Boxing is full of traditions, it needs them, to separate it from other things – you ever notice the shoes boxers wear, the ribbons around their waists, even the amateurs? If you're going to try to murder someone, well, you've got to admit, ribbons are a nice touch.

Anyway, it was the city's amateur Christmas tournament, they did it every year. Usually, the city'd have a big pro fight one weekend in December, and the kids and local amateurs would get to have a go in a city tournament that week, sort of share the limelight in a distant sort of way.

8   The Problem with the Seventh Year

In any case, there was no professional fight that year. Who knows. Maybe someone forgot. But they had the amateur tournament anyway. Like Christmas Eve with no Christmas. People were disappointed.

They didn't know what they were in for.

I'd been invited. By post. They had class.

It took two fights on Thursday to get me into Friday's final. First one was easy. He'd been sparring with the wrong people.

I tried not to laugh, but there you are.

Second fight was a bit more. The guy was strong, bit of a bully. He threw a jab, followed by a hook. Never really knew where the hook was coming from: sometimes left-right, sometimes double-up on the left.

I looked at him between rounds, when we were sitting across from each other. I could tell he thought he had me. But I knew. I mean my coach knew, he told me:

'Straight shots travel faster than hooked punches.'

There's a lot of truth to that, I think. But straight shots are useless if you're going backwards: you got to wade in, go forward into the guy, get hit but unload. It's good, you're afraid – left – right – left – you just let them go. But stepping forward is the problem.

The hard part.

To tell truth, I don't remember much about that fight. I won on points and was into the light middleweight finals.

That made me happy. I knew who it was. I hadn't seen him the day before, but I'd heard about him being there.

Gregory.

I would see him again in the traditional way. A rematch.

I couldn't sleep all night. Had a bit of a headache. But it was more excitement.

Or fear.

I kept thinking about all the things I was going to do to him, you know, the combinations I was going to throw. I was planning them out, one after the other.

I was thinking too much.

I remembered our first fight as well. That feeling.

I couldn't sleep.

Listen, I was eager, it's true, I know I was eager, but there was something there, something else that was spooking me out. Something was always spooking me out.

That night it was the streetlight outside my bedroom window. When I pulled the blind at night I still couldn't sleep.

That streetlight outside made my whole room orange. I hated it.

So I hung a blanket over the window, tucking it in at the top so it would hang down. The orange light still came in around the edges, you know, but that blanket was black.

I lay on my bed and couldn't stop staring at that black square over my window. It just hung there. Blocking everything. So still.

Like a mouth.

I dug out my abnormal psychology textbooks, see what was wrong with me, but wouldn't you know I had every damn disease in the book – you know how they describe symptoms: 'feelings of disorientation,' 'headaches,' 'sleeplessness,' 'intruding thoughts' – I had everything in the whole book.

When it's 2 a.m. and you've convinced yourself you're a paranoid-obsessive-compulsive-bipolar-schizo with a penchant for rough sex, well, you know it's going to be one of those nights.

By the way, this is not the way one usually prepares for a big fight.

I don't know why I went into medicine.

It does fuck with your head. That was the whole problem, really, later on. That's what did me in.

They told me I was getting one of the finest educations in America. Don't believe it.

They taught me how to worry. They taught me about consequence – and what was I left with?

(*Bell rings/lights change.*)

I woke up late the next day. That helped.

When I got to the town hall, I could hear all the people in the streets around it. I could hear voices coming out of the nearby bars, out of bars all the way down the street, even voices halfway across the city.

All the voices were talking about the fights, it was like they say, there was a buzz about the place.

And that made me confident. That was just what I needed.

Looking back, that's when I got happy – just before my bout. I sat in a training room while some the other fighters paced around. And I was so still.

I knew I could win.

When my coach came in to get me ready, I could tell he thought something was up with me, but he didn't mind it.

I was sharp on the pads.

I had feet like a rabbit.

I was going to beat him. But not in a brawl, I was going to outbox him. It was going to be clinical, you know?

I went in the doors and could hear a couple of guys from my gym cheer for me. Then I heard a roar. From the crowd. I couldn't understand why, then I realized.

He'd entered the building. They were cheering for him.

He must have had a lot of family. Probably some fucking Catholic, I thought.

We hit the ring at the same time. I felt electric. I felt ready . . . he . . . he looked exactly the same as last time. He was wearing the same colors. The blue top, the black headgear.

His face was very matter-of-fact, business-like, no emotion.

Everything was just as I had imagined it but all of it was real, right in front of me and so . . . different.

It threw me off.

I started getting nervous. I didn't know why.

I could feel my forehead.

My wrists started itching.

The coach pushed me forward to meet with the referee, to face Gregory, and it hit me.

My heart, it palpitated. Almost knocked me off my feet, you know, in my throat, I was spooked, who wouldn't be?

When you think about it, as I did in front of 2,000 people just before taking part in what would become known as the dirtiest fight in the history of the city, there's no reason for your heart to beat, it just does.

But if you can hold your breath and stop breathing, why not clench your teeth and make your heart stop as well?

I was in bad shape.

It was brilliant.

I think it was the best night of my life.

There I was, Gregory staring me down in the middle of the ring, and all I can think about is whether the mitral valve of the heart might actually be a conscious reflex.

But, you see, thirty seconds later I didn't care.

I was in there.

And it was getting ugly. Fast.

But I stopped thinking. The second right hand he hit me with took care of the thinking, made my head feel like battered pennies.

Once I took that right hand I wanted to kill him.

He could block my jab well, too well, and let's face it, if you can't jab your opponent, you're fucked.

So in the first round I hit him low. The referee warned me but, worse, Gregory didn't say a thing. Didn't look bothered.

Twenty seconds later, I caught him with an elbow and didn't get a flicker.

Then I stamped on his toes and he swore at me. So I stamped on his toes all night!

You see he gave it away. He was angry, unlike anything in that first fight.

In the second round I started throwing the right hand followed by a left hook and left knee at the same time. He didn't like those. Started moving backwards.

I could see myself winning. And I wasn't imagining it. It was right there. When you go from one to the other, it feels quite nice, especially in front of all those people.

Most of which I think were mad at me.

They were jeering.

Someone said, 'I'm going to rip your dick off, you cheating cunt!'

Well, we've all heard that before.

It's just talk.

And they could all fuck off.

I was doing it. I had both hands in it.

That third round . . . it must have been difficult for people to watch.

Everything went.

Everything. We spat, punched low, hit and held, butted, gouged.

He'd lost his cool. I didn't know where I was.

After a minute Gregory knocked the referee down as we wrestled.

At one point, we stood toe-to-toe in the center of the ring and tried to strangle each other.

Every rule in the book was broken at least twice.

He won the bout on points.

But he was nothing special.

The city reporter said that 'for roughness, disregard of ring rules and ethics, and wild fighting, this bout surpassed anything in the history of the city's boxing scene, amateur or professional.'

Gregory's trainer got in the article too, he said, 'It was like there was no referee in the fight. He was holding my boy by the head and banging away at his eyes!'

I was quoted as saying 'I thought I fought a clean fight!'

My own trainer was furious with me. Furious. And after the tournament he found that referee and grabbed him by the collar: 'Why didn't you stop that fight, you dumb fuck!'

'I wanted to,' said the referee, 'but the fight was so vicious, I was afraid that if I stopped it the two boys would have started a race riot.'

'But that boy wasn't black!' My coach screamed, 'both them boys are white!'

'I know,' said the referee, 'but there were a lot of blacks in there, watching. They were all cheering for that other boy. I'm sorry.'

So there you have it: the dirtiest fight in the history of the city, where two white boys almost started a race riot between them.

I went home and stared at my black cloth on the window, the orange light behind it, and . . . I felt thirsty.

I had my first beer in six months and felt better.

I knew I wouldn't be fighting for a while.

Neither would Gregory.

The Amateur Boxing Association wouldn't just let all that slide.

Gregory was suspended from the ring for five months.

I received a suspension for life, but someone told me I'd get reinstated in six to eight months, if I kept my mouth shut.

That suited me fine. I had some prelim exams to get ready for anyway.

I could use a break.

Then the ABA told me they suspended me for life to protect me, that after a performance like that every club in the city would be out to get me.

I told them to fuck off.

Life was easier then. I knew I wanted to be a boxer.

The problem was I wasn't good enough. I knew that – and in truth, I never would be. I was twenty and had been boxing for seven years.

And there was my other life to think about. I was, after all, training to be a general physician.

At least that's the specialty I marked on my application.

And it wasn't going very well. After Christmas, it got worse.

I left the hospital rotations to shadow a physician in his office at the Department of Health, the public clinic for poor people and cheapskates. Sit in with his patients. I could always tell it wouldn't work out.

Help people? If you saw how the Department of Health works, think again.

Each patient gets ten minutes.

Some wealthy fucker who's looking to save a buck walks through the door and gives an exposition on how his little finger hurts and it's interfering with his piano playing, and he gets sent to free physical therapy.

But some poor woman comes in, with a pain in her back and a thick accent, and she can't explain anything, except that it hurts.

Could just be too much booze, judging by her cheeks.

But going over symptoms is useless. A woman like that needs some time, you know? And you think maybe you can help her, really help her – that this is what it's all about.

Ten minutes and they're out the door. You can't explain your problem, out you fucking go with some aspirin. Really. It makes you sick – that woman needed some help.

So I told the doctor's secretary to get her fucking scheduling book in order.

Next thing you know, the doctor walks in and asks why she's crying.

She explained very elegantly that I was a bastard, 'emotional abuse' or some such shit.

The doctor told me to stop it, 'cease and desist' he says. There was something about a warning, and basic procedure.

He'd read my file and told me there was 'nothing to get too upset about here.'

I said if he knew what he was talking about, I might believe him.

That I didn't like the way he talked to patients.

He started talking to me like he talks to them.

Leaning real close in my face like, sounding soft and serious when I knew I was just getting some of the same old shit.

So I kicked him in the balls.

He looked like he enjoyed it. I saw it as a mutually beneficial action – he was smiling after all.

An hour later I was in front of the Dean. It seemed everything on his desk was made of brass.

His balls were probably brass as well, I would like to have kicked them, but he scared the shit out of me.

He'd read the local papers.

He knew about the amateur Christmas tournament.

He was on and on about 'purpose,' the 'general purpose' and my own in particular.

He kept talking about me in the third person. Like I wasn't even there.

Before I knew it, I was promising him I'd behave. He assigned me to a new rotation back at the hospital and said he was cutting me a break.

That was one of the toughest times.

I was in that hospital night and day, haunting all of its white rooms gone rotten.

I would read the paper, and the days just passed. I'd look out the window, and had nothing more to do than anyone else walking by.

I no longer had the fear of going down the gym. That fearful excitement that you better have your shit together by 5:45 p.m. because you were getting in the ring.

I was bored. And I thought, maybe this was a mistake – what was I after? In the grand scheme of things I wasn't much of a boxer, and I'd really come to hate medicine. I admitted that to myself one day in emergency room. I just couldn't see myself as a doctor.

After that I felt better. And was able to carry on with medicine, on different terms.

Unfortunately, after that everything else was different, too, because the very next morning – I saw him again.

Gregory.

And that was the big mistake.

He was the one who first planted the big idea in my head. Even if things went wrong later on, deep down, it's my fault.

Not for what I did, but because after the Christmas tournament I stopped thinking about Gregory, so I stopped looking for him.

And there he was.

Working the cash register of some corner store in the wrong part of town. I'd stopped in to buy some chewing gum.

And when I put my Trident on the counter I saw Gregory behind the register. My eyes must have been out of my head. I think it was more embarrassing than the fight.

But he smiled. Asked me my name.

He knew who I was.

He said he'd been looking for me.

No shit.

But it was weird, he looked like he was genuinely glad to see me. I felt . . . welcome in his presence.

He tried to make small talk, but I just rattled the change in my hand.

It was then that he planted the idea in my head.

He said his boxing club needed a cutman.

Well I was only a medical student and not a very good one but he said he knew that already and it was alright.

I said I couldn't get a license to be a cutman. He said that was alright, too.

He said to quit my club and go down to his. I'd learn more, he said.

He was persuasive, you know, one of them.

I'd learn how to box proper and there were three or four professionals down at his club and I could make a bit on the side as their cutman.

Now, I didn't know anything about being a *cutman*, but I was bored with the hospital and didn't think I'd ever get to box again.

That's when Gregory offered me fifty dollars.

Now it didn't take a genius to see his whole club was after me, that they all probably wanted to kill me, that going down to his club was like a death wish.

He caught my face, caught my eye. 'You're scared,' he said. Not as a question – 'You're scared?' – but as a fully formed statement of fact.

I looked back at him. He said, 'I'll take care of you down there. There are good boys down there. You'll enjoy it.' Enjoy it! And he winks at me!

I told him I hadn't boxed since Christmas. I said I was still suspended. He said that was alright.

He had a goddam answer for everything!

I left the store with directions to his club.

And fifty bucks.

Never got the chewing gum, though.

I knew what was happening.

In two weeks I was as good as ever. Better, because I was sparring with the best in the city, a couple were genuine professionals, some were top city amateurs, a couple were reformed barefisters, others were just plain thugs, or worse.

And there was Gregory.

It was like World War Three every day.

Clean. It was all clean fighting, but they didn't cut me no breaks. They'd come at me, and I'd meet them.

It was a big, unwashed place down on Lamont Avenue. Lots of people from the neighborhood would come and sit there for hours, just watching.

There was even a counter near the entrance that sold tea, sandwiches, lemonade and adhesive tape and bandages, as well as raw eggs – which were a favorite of everyone, even the trainers.

And I didn't sense any anger from them, it was funny.

That was all ancient history.

But I could tell they talked about me. When I wasn't around, or on the other side of the gym. I was something to talk about.

And it wasn't the Christmas tournament. It was because I was there on a deal.

Their cutman, Rod, was going to break me in before he moved to Florida.

(*Bell rings/lights change.*)

Thursday night fights in a big sports center over in Marlboro, east of the city. Professionals. Low-level professionals.

My job was looking after the bucket – a fiver a fight – which I learned was hard enough – bottle here, ice there, not too much ice.

Rod had to work around the head trainer, who would get right in the boxer's face, and this trainer's only got sixty seconds between rounds to be nursemaid, general, and comforting friend while a surgeon's reaching around working on the guy's face.

And when you subtract the time spent getting in and out of the ring, they actually had little more than forty seconds to get that guy ready.

It's beautiful, it really is.

Rod could close six cuts in a minute without looking bothered, get that kid back in the fight, and the presence of mind he had, along with that other corner man.

Where others might panic, they had to say and do the right thing.

When Rod fell ill, I got a call straight from the trainer, Marcus.

I had already put a kit together from stuff in the hospital. And at night I'd arrange it in my little box in different ways, see what was best. I wanted each piece of equipment to be in a predetermined place – Vaseline, cotton buds, gauze, scissors, various coagulants.

I wanted to know where to get my stuff without thinking.
You've got to be prepared. So that day I kept opening
that box at the hospital and making sure everything was
in position, so that bing! Cut. Automatic. Bing, bing. You
know. Bing, bing! And I'm ready to go.

I even slipped some things from the ER into the box that
I shouldn't have.

But it all came in useful.

In the first round I thought they were going to stop the fight.
This kid's nose was like a faucet. His skin cut like pastry.

I already had four cotton buds covered in adrenaline when
he came over after the first. Stuck two up each nostril.

It was ugly to watch. He was getting hit everywhere.

After the third I was putting ice on his neck and his shorts
and everywhere else.

Marcus is screaming at him: 'Box! Box! Box! That's it. Now
get outta there! I told you, I don't like fighters who get hit!'

But this guy won me over. He was a flatnosed, tough kid,
and you could tell by the way he fought, he was prideful
as hell.

Then there was the seventh. Both boxers' heads came
together, and when they broke, blood was gushing down
our fighter's nose – but not out of his nostrils.

His nose had been ripped lengthwise.

The bell rang.

He came into the corner, and I got a look at it. The gash was
so deep it looked like he had two noses. Split like a walnut.

What the hell could I do? Marcus, the trainer, wasn't even
speaking. He just stood there, looking at *me*.

Marcus looked like he'd just shat himself, come to
think of it.

But then things just started to happen. The kind of things you can be proud of.

I sat the boy down and reached in my bag. I took out something nobody else uses to close wounds. I used Monsel's solution, that I'd slipped into my kit that day.

It was dangerous stuff, but they use it in the ER when people's arms get cut off, stuff like that.

It coagulates blood all right. It's like pouring cement into someone.

I put some right down the middle of his nose, pressed it back together, and I knew this fight couldn't last much longer.

Marcus just stood there looking stupid so I said, 'Listen, you better go out there and knock this cunt out before the ring doctor stops the fight.'

And that's just what he did. He was so proud, he looked at me and then just went out there and did it.

Marcus was ecstatic, thrilled with me. He started putting the word around, telling people I was 'a real doctor.'

That actually made me pretty happy, although when I heard about it, I realized I had skipped the hospital three days in a row.

I was getting really sloppy with my course.

I usually tried to make my absences more subtle, cut my days short.

But people at the hospital could tell I was out when I should have been in.

When I was late or cutting out early.

Allusions were made.

It started getting to me. I had scraped by my prelims but had a lot of ground to make up at the hospital. I started missing training sessions down at the gym.

One day, after having been away too long, I got in the
ring with this thug and came out with two black eyes
and a cut that started at the corner of my lip and ended
in the middle of my cheek, made me look like I was
always smiling.

It was like it was intentional, like the head trainer was
letting me know I was expected at that club every day or
not at all.

I couldn't do any more sparring until the cut healed.

Gregory had just gone professional and I was on
forced holiday.

What's worse, I started spooking patients at the hospital –
when someone with two black eyes and an artificially
extended mouth comes to look at your charts, you wonder
if you haven't already died and are now having some evil
spirit decide which room in hell suits you best.

My supervisor told me to take a week off, pull
myself together.

(*Bell rings/lights change.*)

After a couple of days staring at the wall with nothing to do,
I decided there was only one action left to take: go out on
the town and live a little. Enjoy myself a bit.

Not as easy as it sounds. Fun and relaxing, sure, but for
me it was more like trying to fly a kite when you don't have
any arms.

I mean, I can't tell you what I was like back then. It was sad.

I hated everyone. It's just the way it was.

I'd meet someone, and they were a shithead, just like
that. And the thing was, they always hated me back.
I could tell. Their half-looks punctuating every other
demeaning gesture.

But you know what? I was alright with that.

The people getting in my way on the sidewalk. The Gook I bought my pornos from. Nurses.

They all hated me. And that suited me fine because I didn't like them anyway.

Even if I didn't know them.

I mean, I was like Scrooge . . . just, you know, without any money.

Now I had a *little* cash in my pocket from working them fights, and I finally went out to have a good time – a four-day bender. I'd never been on one and they seemed to have a lot to recommend them.

However, I didn't get to the bottom of my second beer when I met Ruthie.

I was just sitting there, and asked her if I could have a look at her newspaper. She looked up at me and I could see the shock in her eyes from my own hideousness.

Like she couldn't look away because it was too interesting, that strange cut coming out of my mouth and across my face, the bruised eyes.

I asked her right away if I could buy her a drink. No hesitation at all, BAM! Just like that I asked her.

She looked like a stunned deer. And said yes. She'd love a cup of coffee.

I said don't you like beers?

She said it was still morning and her shift was starting soon.

You just can't argue with a woman like that.

Then she put on this cap, this black cap, with her dark hair and high collar; she kind of looked like a toy soldier, the smiling ones with pink circles in their cheeks, and I said, 'Are you a chauffeur or something?'

She worked on the trains, clipping people's tickets on the north routes that run all the way up to Gloucester and Portsmouth. I smiled, the stitches on my lips and cheek tightening around my grin, and I joked if she would let me ride north with her out to the coast, to the beaches, for free.

She was looking at me like I was one of those hideously deformed people who, in their own way, are also very sweet.

She didn't know I was serious.

I liked that about her.

Before you know it I'm on the train with her and leaving that city behind. She said 'hi' to me every time she walked through the carriage. I was preoccupied if she was her normal self or making extra trips back and forth just to see me.

One time she stops short and says, 'Are you really a medical student?' I showed her my hospital ID and she walked away looking very impressed.

Then I popped into the toilet and caught a look at myself in the mirror.

I got off at the shoreline alone. But when the train pulled away a hand came out through the window and waved. Who else could it have been?

That sand felt good between my toes. I thought I must be pretty damn handsome if I could have a slapped-up face and still press a girl's buttons.

There was no one around and I suddenly remembered it was the end of February.

But I wanted to cleanse myself, so I went into the ocean. It was cold, and I just floated, until I stopped moving and the sea dragged me. It didn't feel good until I got back out on the beach, laid myself down, just me in my wet pants lying on the beach.

I smelt the sea, not in general but on *me*. The smell you get only when you come out of the water.

Then I knew I would be alright because of that smell, the feeling it reminded me of . . . And that relaxed me. In its own way. I knew that if I put my head down against the Fear I would be alright.

(*Pause. Bell rings/lights change.*)

Some evenings, I'd work five fights. My sleeves would be blood right up to the armpits.

But I had developed my own system of doing things: I'd bring into the corner a pail, sponge, bottle and supply of ice . . . the coagulants, a bottle of smelling salts, a little brandy and a mixture of honey and lemon.

The brandy stimulates the heart without intoxicating, honey supplies energy and lemon juice chases away the nauseous feeling a fighter gets when he's tired.

I never used Monsel's solution again. It was too dangerous, for the boxer, and for me, too. I still had a medical career to think about.

Mostly I used adrenaline to stop the blood. When a guy had it bad, I'd mix in a venom solution as well.

After that, all I could do was pray for a lucky punch.

(*Bell rings/lights change.*)

I could tell Ruthie was interested. She asked me lots of questions about medicine, what kind of doctor I was going to be, if I'd ever considered pediatrics . . . And you know something? Medicine seemed a lot more interesting when I was talking to her about it.

Telling her how an MRI works felt like foreplay. It was almost enough to make me glad I was a medical student.

On the day I was fully healed, the day I had all the stitches removed, I asked her out.

She said she had a boyfriend.

I said I don't give a fuck.

She asked me if that's why I got beaten up. She told me to watch out because her boyfriend knew Tae Kwan Do, or Tai Kee, or Duck Fang Doo or some such shit.

She was so nice Ruthie. Trying to warn me.

But like most really nice people, when I got to know her, I found out she was ruthless. Completely.

I asked her on a date, and she said I could take her swimming sometime at the YMCA.

I mean of all the things to say. I refused.

She said we'd be safe there from her boyfriend.

So I dragged her to the cinema. I insisted on taking her out to dinner. After some pushing and shoving, I got to take her to the carnival when it came to town.

And I never saw her boyfriend. I think that was her way of saying she'd meet me without having to call it a date.

I had some money and we'd go out the way people our age had always heard about it being done. But she never let me kiss her. She was ruthless like that. It was like she was being pure but there was something cruel in it.

Sometimes standing on the bus, I'd put my arm around her to steady her.

One time I was walking up to the hospital and ran into her: she came up behind me and she squeezes me, her mouth hitting my neck in some kind of ambiguous way.

That was when she asked me if I'd go to a party at her house. It was for her grandfather's eightieth birthday. Her whole family would be there.

I thought I was in!

But of course that was silly, as I realized the way it was going to be between us. Not too significant, you could say. Not much to say, despite my numerous attempts. I felt like a novelty in her life, just because I wore a stethoscope around my neck every day and was a 'medical student.'

I was entertaining for her.

(*Bell rings/light change.*)

I hadn't gone back to boxing myself, I kept putting it off for some reason or other.

But it wasn't long before I got beaten up again anyway.

I was working in a 200-seater above some bar for Marcus. Our guy must have been in his forties.

He was a funny one. Strange.

When I was looking him over just before the fight, he told me he thought he had syphilis.

He just blurted it out. Just like that.

Like he'd been dying to tell someone.

I told him we could discuss it later.

I should have known he'd enjoy hitting his opponent below the belt.

He did it almost immediately after the opening bell.

When he did it again in the third, it looked like some kind of uppercut to the testicles.

The other fella went down but got up again.

The crowd was none too pleased. They were mostly for the other guy.

When it happened again in the next round, his opponent didn't get up.

The crowd went wild.

In a moment the coaches had poured into the action and started hitting one another. The rest of the cornermen weren't far behind, including me, and neither were about thirty spectators.

The whole ring was one giant brawl.

I was hitting some guy in the face and didn't know why.

I remember getting the feeling that everyone else knew each other, from the same housing project or something, and had jumped in the ring at the first chance to settle some old scores.

But why was I hitting this guy in the head? What was my reason?

In any case, I walked away with bruises covering my face like big polka dots.

I looked like a black and blue leper or something.

Understandably, my enthusiasm for this job suddenly started to wane.

And the birthday party for Ruthie's grandfather was that weekend. She told me to wear a jacket and tie, so the first thing I did was go out and buy a new suit.

I thought it would help distract attention away from my face.

I don't think Ruthie's mother knew what to say when she opened the door – I was in a $200 suit and my face looked like a train wreck had just shat on it.

Too many introductions followed. Her uncle took one look at me and asked if I'd been in Vietnam. Then he laughed. I think it was some kind of joke.

I kept wishing someone would open a window or turn down the heater but they just took turns filling my glass and talking at me.

It was so humid.

Ruthie kept telling everyone how I was a 'medical student,' I wanted to smack her and tell her to shut up.

Things got worse when we sat down to dinner: I was placed next to Ruthie's aunt, who'd married into money in Connecticut. Before I knew it I was talking about horses.

She had kept her tight figure. She was right about everything.

Seriously, she had two jobs, three kids, and was doing a doctorate.

And drank a hell of a lot.

When I asked her about her thesis, she said, 'Oh dear, I'll spare you the details, after all it's very difficult and very boring.'

For a moment I thought she wanted me to pry it out of her.

But before I could think of anything clever to say, she started babbling about language and thought.

She was one of those people who could talk in a real sophisticated way without saying very much, but her thesis was something like: 'abstract thought isn't possible without language,' because if you couldn't articulate an idea, it didn't exist.

For her research she taught some kids from the projects, who proved her point.

No one said they were capable of abstract thought, because they were ill-educated and illiterate and because, as she put it, 'Daddy comes home drunk every Friday night and slams their head into a radiator.'

The way she said it, it was like an insult to people who get their heads slammed into radiators.

But she was sticking up for these kids.

She proved they were capable of abstract thought, and in turn they proved her thesis: clearly it was the spoken language these children knew that enabled abstraction.

She'd proved it through a variety of tests on them that demonstrated the reflex between language and thought, even amongst such 'ignorant, illiterate specimens.'

I asked her about what tests she gave these kids. There were loopholes in it, I said.

She just drank more wine, like she was trying to end the conversation.

I said disproving her theory was easy.

Just take those same kids to a swimming pool, on a beautiful summer day.

They'd have lots of fun in the water. Playing games.

Then, without warning or explanation, pick a child and pull him to the bottom of the deep end. Hold him down there, very still.

He'll try to get away, but you just hold him there tight, no matter how much he struggles.

When he's near passing out, you bring him to the surface long enough for him to take one deep breath, then drag him back down to the bottom.

You'll find, as you hold him down there twenty feet underwater, where nothing is spoken, no words exchanged, that he stops trying to get away, and sits there in your tensed arms without giving you any trouble.

That he accepts it. Is no longer afraid of what you're going to do.

It's very quiet down there after all. He stops panicking.

So you stick a knee into his chest.

Watch his face, the shock, and pain. Later the acceptance, that he can handle it.

That he's capable of not worrying, even about your knee in his chest. Even about . . . drowning. Isn't that a beautiful thing?

'And I'll tell you fucking what,' I said. 'There's no language involved in any of it. But it's a pretty fucking abstract experience, you know? It's thinking without thinking, without language way down there in the water.

So I'd say you're pretty far off the fucking mark, aren't you?'

She was just staring at me, her glass at her lips. She looked petrified.

When I didn't speak, she started following the bruises on my face like a game of connect-the-dots.

It started making me nervous, so I told her these were just things I'd read about in books.

Ruthie sat down on the other side of me. She was like an oasis in the desert.

'Are you having a nice time?' She asked.

'Lovely.'

She touched my ear, then felt the lapel of my new suit.

It was a moment I should have enjoyed a bit more, I guess.

(*Bell rings. Light change – various shades of chlorine blue move about the stage, ideally making it appear as if* **Man** *is at the bottom of a swimming pool.*)

When God came down to Moses, He said that every seventh year the land must bear no fruit, and remain uncultivated in tribute to the Lord.

As soon as He said this, the people began to worry, and ask the Lord what they were supposed to eat in the year of famine.

God replied that the crops from the sixth year would have to feed them through the seventh.

A raw deal, in more ways than one. Because the people had been *told*, they worried about it. From the first year to the sixth, they wondered if they would survive.

They spent lots of time planning ahead.

They thought if they didn't worry and prepare, they would starve.

Would it have been so bad not to know about the seventh year? Or even, not to care?

You know, when they made it to year eight, I bet they wondered why they spent all that time worrying. After they had made it through.

What's not written down there in Leviticus, is that if they had heard about the oncoming famine, and not cared, they might have made it through the seventh year anyway.

Years one to six might have been a walk in the park, and seventh year not so bad.

They might have been fine, after all.

But once you learn God's language, and he speaks to you, is it possible not to listen?

Once you're stuck into medicine, is it possible to stop thinking? Can you stop looking for symptoms – or signs of the next disaster?

(*Bell rings. lights back to normal.*)

When Ruthie's family got up from the table, it was time for me to go home.

Gregory was waiting for me there.

He hadn't spoken to me in a couple of months. Too busy.

He asked all the normal questions, came up for a cup of coffee. I knew he'd stopped in to size me up.

He'd heard the rumor that I told Marcus and the rest of them to fuck off after the fight last week.

Gregory took one look at my face and said I'd shown myself to be a strong healer in the past, and I'd be back in no time.

I never wanted to see Gregory, Marcus, or any of them ever again.

I was finished! No more boxing gyms. I was a future doctor and needed to start acting like one, for Christ's sake.

Wouldn't you know that's when Gregory started coming by a lot?

Sometimes, he'd just walk into my apartment, and I'd be sleeping on the sofa or something and he wouldn't even wake me up, just sit down at the table and read his paper.

He'd wake me up with one of his farts or something and I'm like, 'Christ Almighty! What are you doing here?'

He'd just talk to me. Normal stuff.

I told him about Ruthie, that she made me happy. I told him I was thinking of becoming a pediatrician. He nodded.

A few weeks later he says I'm wanted down the club.

Then I knew he'd talk about me getting back on the horse again and all that.

Worst of all, I knew he was right.

Gregory had that way about him, persuasive. I felt like he was looking out for me.

But I didn't do anything, except put Gregory, and the rest of them, off as long as I could.

Until it happened. Gregory came upstairs and woke me up. Said he'd just signed for his fourth professional fight, and wanted me to be his cutman.

He tried to pay me in cash then and there.

I said I'd do it for free.

Two weeks later I was back in the corner rubbing linament into a cut and looking forward to Gregory's fight.

He'd won his first three pro fights easy, and now he was facing an old journeyman from Ireland. Quality fighter, though, the kind you have to beat to begin making a name for yourself as a professional.

It wouldn't be a walkover. But I was sure Gregory would win.

I watched him train.

He had that way, you know, he'd get to the gym early, do his handwraps real steady, not rush anything, bring his own Vaseline to the gym and put it on steady, warm up steady, get in the ring, and go totally mental.

He was shredding guys. Knocking them out in training.

As nice a guy as he was, he didn't feel bad about it, either.

He was ready.

(*Bell rings/lights change.*)

Then I heard something through Marcus. Something Gregory didn't know about his opponent. This Irishman had a reputation. He was more than just a journeyman. He was one of those.

You could hit him.

He'd let you hit him.

A real problem, especially among older fighters. They get so used to taking the punches, they walk right into them without being bothered.

Often trainers force fighters like that to retire. It gets ugly. But if they knew how to punch back while getting hit, it made them very dangerous.

Unless you really knew what you were doing they would knock you out. That's it. How they made a living.

His record was less than stellar, and that's all anyone in the gym knew.

So.

Marcus and I weren't going to say anything about it to Gregory, or anyone else.

We weren't stupid. Besides, Gregory had never been in better form.

Some boxers tire of the drudgery, of the roadwork and sparring and weights.

For Gregory, it was dynamite.

(*Bell rings/lights change.*)

No fighter is truly calm before a bout. We all have our different methods of dealing with the Fear. Everything seems different, inside of your body and outside of you, too. That inside is moving on you. The outside looks different, but the inside . . .

For Gregory, it was about getting everything ready nice and early, down to the last detail, and then he wanted to be left alone.

The fight was being held in Trenton, where Gregory's bout would be the undercard of an undercard.

We were three hours early getting to the big venue.

No one was around.

I was dreaming about Ruthie, she was coming that night to watch. She wanted to see me in action.

We got everything out and in perfect order. Then Gregory lay down on the table and Tilly and I went around the corner for some dinner.

Tilly was Gregory's trainer, and a mean son of a bitch.
I never liked him.

Tilly was the kind of guy who would steal pennies off the
eyes of dead men.

He asked me why I hadn't started boxing again yet.

I said I didn't know.

He asked me if I'd heard anything about this Irishman.

I said I hadn't.

He looked at me, and said: 'Good.'

(*Bell rings/light change.*)

Should I have said something?

Would it have made a difference?

It could have made things worse. Gregory, at least, didn't
look afraid going into the bout.

Early in the first round he knocked the Irishman backwards
with a left hook. You could hear the rattle of his head.

But he shook it off.

He was counter-punching Gregory, but when Gregory
threw shots, sometimes this Irishman didn't bother trying
to slip punches before retaliating.

He'd just take them, and clobber Gregory with left hooks
or straight rights.

The bell rang and Tilly seemed really confident. 'Throw
your shots and get the hell out of there,' he kept saying,
'this guy's got an empty tank, get on him for four rounds
and he'll fall over – he'll quit like the bully he is.'

Gregory was relentless, always diving in with his shots –
left – right – left – with speed and above all with power.
But sometimes he was getting caught on the way in.

Otherwise the Irishman would just take punches and move forward. He was bleeding over his eye after the third but didn't look winded.

He was never on his toes. It was more like he walked around the ring.

Gregory came into the corner looking slightly battered but as intense as ever. He didn't want to listen to anyone, he was warm and he was going to take care of business.

There was a big crowd, going nuts. They could smell something.

I started thinking Gregory might not win. Problem was, he didn't have any other style of fighting, besides going right at his opponent.

What's wrong with that?

He was blessed with tremendous power in his punches.

And a big pair of balls.

But this Irishman knew that the difference between getting knocked out and being grazed by a punch was often a quarter of an inch, and he knew that quarter of an inch the way only truly experienced fighters can.

And when he did get caught by a big punch, he just threw the right hand straight back into Gregory's face.

Still, our trainer looked happy. Gregory was, after all, clearly the more fit of the two.

But his right eye started to swell badly.

'This guy's nothing but a puncher,' Tilly kept telling him, 'you got to play checkers with him, think!'

A round later Gregory's nose was broken and bleeding badly.

But still, the trainer was happy, 'You've got to up your work rate, lad, get on him and he'll fold. He's a tulip, I'm telling you.'

Gregory had a good round after that. He just kept coming forward and meeting his opponent.

The Irishman took some brutal shots, and started dropping his hands. He started throwing big hooks from his waist, and taking more punishment.

You've got to take punishment to give punishment, and this guy wasn't missing his chance to dish it out. But he was trading in quantity for quality, and that's not going to win the judges over in a decision.

Gregory was definitely ahead on points.

But when he got knocked down at the end of the seventh, I thought I was going to vomit. The Hippocratic oath was ringing in my ears.

I felt physically ill.

Gregory's right eye was swollen shut.

I only had sixty seconds to ice both his eyes. It wasn't long enough.

He was moving differently, swaying back and forth and coming in from the sides instead of straight at the other guy.

Like his legs were wobbly.

The trainer kept yelling for Gregory to double-up his jab, like that would solve everything.

But Gregory couldn't jab, because the Irishman knew something nobody knows anymore, how to clinch.

You can't hold on to your opponent in boxing but this guy knew the proper way to put his hands on the outside of Gregory's chest and maneuver him.

He started spinning Gregory into the corner or against the ropes.

Or just pulling him close for some good in-fighting.

Every time Gregory tried to pull away and fight orthodox, this bastard would pull him back in and start cracking him with a hook or uppercut.

It was slow but they were all big shots.

This was all very clever stuff.

The Irishman was tall as well. When he clinched, his head became a weapon out there. They should have put a glove on it.

When the bell rang, I had to lead Gregory back to the corner. I wasn't sure he could see at all.

His right eye was so swollen it had to be lanced and drained. I went to his left eye where the upper lid was split wide open.

I was still working when the bell rang. There were two rounds left, but now I was sure the referee was going to stop the fight. Any moment. It was the only reasonable thing to do!

I started getting spooked.

It went on and on. I realized they would probably finish the round, but that doesn't mean it was still a fight. That Irishman had Gregory clinched tight, like the ring was a spider web.

Gregory was taking everything and seeing none of it.

The noise of the crowd shook my ice bucket.

I couldn't believe that thirty-five minutes ago Gregory had looked the picture of health: strong, clean, excited, magnificent.

His battered face now looked terribly vague. Why was I the only one to notice?

In every clinch the Irishman had him at his mercy. Gregory was struggling just to get away.

I told Tilly this was crazy.

'He's ahead on points,' Tilly said. 'The ref is giving Gregory the chance to stay on his feet for two more rounds and cash in. We're lucky.'

The bell rang and Tilly laughed.

'Brilliant, now you just stick and move this round and let's get the hell out of here. You got to dig deep.'

I tried working on Gregory's face but Tilly pushed me away – 'Leave him alone! Let him catch his breath for Christ's sake. He's home free.'

I looked for any kind of flicker in Gregory's eyes. He wasn't doing much besides breathing.

I asked him what my name was.

He just moaned at me.

I asked him where he was.

The moan was fainter. Like it wasn't even a word.

(*Silence.*)

'It's over,' I said, and walked towards the referee.

Tilly practically tackled me from behind. He had me by the shirt and was screaming me back into the corner.

I stood up straight real slowly.

'Take your goddamned hands off me. He can't take any more. He's defenseless. Get the hell away from me. I'm the boss here. It's over.'

(*Silence.*)

When the door closed behind us it was terribly quiet.

Just the echo of Gregory's heavy, rapid inhalation.

They sat him down against a wall. He looked like shit, but just kept saying faintly, 'I feel fine, I'm fine, I'm fine.'

The ambulance driver had come in and said he wanted to take Gregory to the hospital.

Gregory refused. Politely. But something was wrong.

The ring doctor came in and said Gregory must go to the hospital. It was mandatory procedure when a corner stopped a fight.

'Come along son,' he kept saying.

(*Silence.*)

But Gregory sat still, and just started staring at me.

(*Silence.*)

He was very composed.

His right eye was still shut. It didn't matter: he could see, out of his left eye. I thought his split eyelid had covered it with too much blood.

But it was definitely me he was looking at.

Now everyone noticed. They all stopped talking.

I didn't know what to say. I couldn't move.

His face was an absolute mess but that one wounded eye looking out at me, it was calm and unmoving.

And it wasn't happy.

The ring doctor stood between us and led Gregory away.

Everyone started screaming.

Gregory was their prize horse. I'd fucked it all up.

But didn't they understand?

Hadn't they seen what I'd seen?

(*Three rapid rings of bell.*)

When the men with suits on came into the dressing room,
I was gone: through the door, up the aisle steps, and off
down the corridor.

I could hear feet following me but I was too young for them.

I started looking for Ruthie in the crowd.

Everyone was cheering on the next bout.

In a clamor someone burst onto the arena floor from the
dressing rooms. He was a bloody, near-naked savage, and
started running up and down the aisle stairs, ignoring the
cat-calls of ushers.

So rabid none of them touched him.

Even the crowd got distracted. There was a maniac in
the house.

Gregory.

Looking for me. Looking for blood. Revenge for what
I'd done to him.

Then someone grabbed my hand from behind. Ruthie.
She dragged me out to her van and we took off.

After a while, she turned to me, looking very serious:
'Are you all right?'

(*Bell rings/light change.*)

For hours I stared at my watch, counting out three-minute
rounds, to see how long they were.

Not very long, really. Three minutes goes by quite quickly,
to be honest.

All this time now, and it would take Gregory months to get
that kind of fight again. Maybe a year. Maybe never.

And he'd almost won it the first time.

I started thinking maybe I wasn't a very opportunistic
person. That I was doomed to mediocrity, or worse.

I didn't feel very safe, and it wasn't just that Gregory was out to scalp me now. That they were all going to ruin me.

It was what I'd done. It was the type of person who would do something like that, wreck beautiful achievements out of concern for something called 'consequence.'

Ruthie drove us all the way back to Worcester. She knew I couldn't go back to my apartment.

It was the early hours of the morning and everything seemed empty.

Even the all-night gas station, and there were people inside.

When we parked in front of her house, she asked me to be quiet because of her parents.

We kept the lights off. It was the same sofa though, stiff but friendly.

'Things will be all right,' she kept whispering.

She reached over and touched my fingers. But when I looked at her eyes, she asked me if I wanted a cup of tea. Whenever I looked at her, she would start going on and on about tea.

It was going to happen, I knew it for certain.

There was another silence. A more awkward one.

She smiled, and asked me if I minded sleeping on the sofa.

I nodded and said I didn't mind.

Then she asked me if I'd go to the university tomorrow and try to get a new room there, because I'd be safer on campus.

I nodded. That was probably true.

Then she leaned over and said in her soft, soft voice –

STOP

(*Lights fade to blackout. Silence. Lights suddenly back to full strength.*)

When Ruthie took herself upstairs, I decided to go for a walk and get some fresh air. Actually, I went for a drive.

She deserved to lose her wheels. Two minutes later I was pulling out onto the highway.

I had never driven a van before and didn't like it. Everything echoed inside.

I wondered where I'd go, but knew exactly, you know?

A quick trip around the city, past the hospital real slow, so I could look through the doors of the ER and see if there were any patients in there I knew.

I could remember their eyes, the shape of their faces, like fish who swim too close to the glass.

Then I went north, keeping the railtracks on one side of me.

Back to the beach. It was dark in the water then. I didn't know what was under me.

And it took me a long time, after dropping out, the dead-end jobs that were left for me, never getting married . . .

I think about being in the water that night.

Did I ever come out?

Can you find me?

END

www.ingramcontent.com/pod-product-compliance
Lightning Source LLC
Chambersburg PA
CBHW070014100426
42741CB00012B/3234